HOW
TO
MAKE
A
JOURNAL
OF
YOUR
LIFE

How to make a journal of your life

by d. price

TEN SPEED PRESS
BERKELEY, CALIFORNIA

Published in the United States by Ten Speed Press,
an imprint of the Crown Publishing Group, a division
of Random House, Inc., New York.
www.crownpublishing.com
www.tenspeed.com

Ten Speed Press
and the Ten Speed Press
colophon are registered
trademarks of Random House, Inc.

Library of Congress Cataloging-in-Publication Data
Price, D. (Daniel). 1957-
   How to make a journal of your life / D.Price
      p. cm.
   1. Diaries--Authorship. 2. CreativeWriting.I.Title
PN4390.P75 1999   99-25687
808' .02--dc21   CIP

TIPI

ISBN: 978-1-58008-093-4
Printed in China

Design by Daniel Price

17 16 15 14 13 12 11 10 9 8

First Edition

This book is dedicated to my children Shane and Shilo and their mother Lynne, who came up with the idea for it one night in the sweat lodge.

CONTENTS

acknowledgments

Many <u>BIG</u> thanks and back pats need to go out to all these people who helped me through the fog and the many events that led to this book. Steve Lenn for the ears and inspiration. The Allens for the meadow in which to dream in. Eric Meyer and the <u>SIMPLE</u> gang for the ticket to a bigger world. Peter and Donna at <u>SAKURA</u> for all those sketching pens, <u>SIERRA DESIGNS</u> for the tents, the Gregorys for true friendship, Kurt Holloman for inspiration, and my family for allowing me so much freedom.

THE OLD DODGE

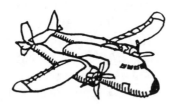

1.
•WALK THE PATH•

Has your intuition been telling you to get an empty journal and begin filling it with all the interesting events of your life? Well, time is racing by. All those neat things that happened just last week have quickly become your past. Lost in all that white noise of our fast paced, modern lifestyles.

So why not begin a new journey today? Find a nice empty book and start what could be the most fascinating and fulfilling activity of your entire life.

old trailer seen while riding a train thru Oregon

So, did you do it yet? Did you decide that yes, your life is valuable and certainly worth recording? Imagine sometime way out there in your future, you'll be able to pull that diary down from a dusty shelf and relive all the details of any given day. You will see connections and patterns and realize more clearly how you got here from there. And not only will this be valuable to you, in the same way that photo albums are, but your immediate family, and especially your own children, will treasure your varied observations of their childhood and lives long after you've passed on.

Now that you have your new journal, i was going to suggest going over to the local tea and coffee spot to fill in your first page. You could write about your move to begin keeping a diary. You could make a sketch of the coffee cup.

2

Maybe you would find a coffee shop a wee bit intimidating? I know i like a private place to work when digging deep into those personal thoughts. So maybe you have come back home, found some quiet music on a radio, sat down

in that big easy chair, and have begun contemplating all those big, white, and very empty journal pages again. Kinda scary huh? Well try not to panic.

You see, your mind will be saying obnoxious things like this: 1. WHAT MAKES YOU THINK YOU HAVE ANYTHING WORTHWHILE TO SAY? 2. THERE'S NOTHING SPECIAL ABOUT YOUR OLD HUMDRUM LIFE THAT WARRANTS DOCUMENTATION. 3. WHO SAID YOU WERE A WRITER ANYWAY? DON'T EMBARRASS YOURSELF. Well, well, that's all real interesting, Mr. Brain. Fortunately we have decided to send you off on sabbatical for awhile and will instead be using our hearts to fill these pages. Heh. Heh.

On hearing this news your heart may begin to beat wildly. It will greatly appreciate you considering it worthy. Goose bumps may appear up and down your spine. And given this new task, the heart says things like this: 1. MY THOUGHTS, DEEDS, AND DOINGS ARE WHO I AM TRYING TO BE, AND EACH ONE IS A GIFT THAT DOES WARRANT RECORDING. 2. IF I GROW TIRED OF SELF-EXAMINATION, ALL I NEED DO IS LIFT MY EYES AND BEHOLD THE BEAUTY OF OUR GLORIOUS WORLD. 3. WRITING DOWN MY OWN THOUGHTS WILL BE THE EASIEST THING IN THE WORLD TO DO BECAUSE I'LL BE EXPRESSING MY OWN INNERMOST FEELINGS, AND ONLY I KNOW WHAT THOSE ARE.

So go ahead and scribble. At first you may dislike your seemingly pretentious babbling. But hey, great novels are not written overnight. Try to do some writing and remember to listen only to your heart, not your head. Then have a cookie.

guy watching the boats going out on oregon coast

4

"I have seldom gone on a tramp without seeing things that made the heart ache with their beauty or pathos, and other things that set the mind a-tingle with intellectual curiosity. I do not refer to great episodes, but to the little things, unexpected visions of life! Some were unforgettable in themselves and seemed to need no other tablets than those of memory, and yet it was a great addition to inner content and happiness to describe them in my day-book of travels." STEPHEN GRAHAM <u>THE GENTLE ART OF TRAMPING</u>

neat plane that landed at our airport last fall

the view from Ted's place

FIND THE WAY

Many folks have gone so far as to actually purchase an empty book, then feverishly embark on a daily schedule of writing in it. Most of these efforts last for only a short while, then fizzle out. Mainly because the author found it necessary to write each and every day, or _else_. Well I don't know about you, but there isn't anything i want to do every day. This school-like attitude would surely kill any creative endeavor. So unless you are filled with huge and fanatical compulsions to document your life, you may want to go slowly, pursuing that ever-so-vague idea that seems to rest just outside your field of vision. Being careful, of course, to avoid rules of any kind. And when there are no more rules about how much time you're supposed to be spending with your journal, and when you feel lighthearted and bouyant about what you want to put in, you'll find yourself enjoying the time and doing good work. Not just making it another addition to your already busy schedule.

While it is true that many and most personal diaries are kept hidden under bedroom pillows, filled with any amount of secret sufferings, I'd like to propose you simply use

view from the backseat of Carl's new plane

any old spiral notebook for those exorcises. This new little empty book you now hold in your hands deserves better than that. Perhaps instead of focusing on negative things, it could have only your enlightened thoughts.

This is all about breaking old boring habits, you see. This is about rejoicement! Noticing that small gesture, or the neatest thing you saw that day, you realize you could make notes about absolutely anything? That everything is just sitting there waiting for you to take notice of it? Does this excite you? Are you now ready to look at the world in a new way? How hard is it to stop your daily running around and spend a few moments just looking and listening, then making a mental note to write about it later on? Or better yet, make a habit of keeping that journal in your pocket or purse

chair drawn from a book about chairs

and instead of burying your face in the morning paper, or evening news, pull out your journal and make some notes about what you see there going on around you. That note will mean a lot more to you in ten years than what the television was spewing out, guaranteed.

Look absolutely anywhere and there are wonders to behold, and if you think otherwise, according to one writer, whose name won't come to me right now, rest assured it is no one's fault but your own. So we can create a good thing if that is our intention. Always remember that your voice and anything

Cow that mooed and was acting mad at us. He was a MAD COW.

you create is uniquely yours. No one else in the entire world can say things quite the way you do. Your own personal being, sitting back in there behind those sparkling eyeballs, has a totally unique perspective on this world, shared by no one else. Spend an hour pretending your eyes are a camera some time, and make mental snapshots of all the cool scenes and things you see. Then go have another cookie.

Shilo's mouse she caught at POINT LOBOS

9

3.
SEARCH AND YOU SHALL FIND

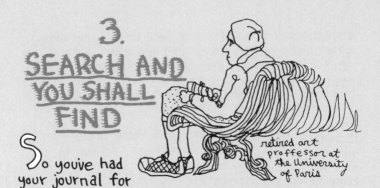

retired art proffessor at the University of Paris

So you've had your journal for awhile. You say you are enjoying keeping track of the special events of your life........but that when you go back to read what you have worked so hard to write, it seems boring. It doesn't seem to ring true. To sing. To uplift. To well, you know, sound good. Like all those wonderful novels you've read. All that great poetry. Those inventive stories that line the shelves of bookstores. <u>HOW</u> DO THEY DO THAT <u>ANYWAY</u>?!

If you do lots of reading you'll begin to feel this way sooner or later. Why do Hemingway's sentences look so elemental yet say so much? How did that Faulkner fellow conjure up such

A L C A T R A Z

an outrageously dreamy world? What is it that makes those mystery novels so darn captivating? Well, think about it. Most books are written by _professional writers_. That's right. People who have practiced and honed character and descriptive skills for years. Of course you're impressed. And having all that literary noise rattling around in your skull can tend to make your own scribblings seem quite insignificant indeed.

Why not stuff all those piles of enticing books right in the back closet

250 million year old fossil from the **DIMETRODON** more closely related to us humans than any dinosaur!

for awhile, and spend some time learning to listen to _your own_ voice? Where is your own voice? You may ask. Well it talks to you each and every day. And you can bet that's your voice scrawled out in the angry journal you keep hidden in the nightstand. So lure it out. Relax with a cool drink on the porch and see what positive, life-affirming bits and pieces it might have to share.

"It is in description that the keeper
of a diary becomes artist. All description is art, and in describing an
event, an action or a being, you enter
into the joy of art. You are more than
the mere secretary of life, patiently
taking down dictation; you become its
singer, the expresser of its glory.
With a verbal description goes also
sketching, the thumbnail sketch, the
vague impression. There is no reason
for being afraid of bad drawing in
one's own personal travel diary. The
main thing is that it be yours and have
some relationship to the eyes and the
thing seen."
STEPHEN GRAHAM
THE GENTLE ART OF TRAMPING

Shane having hot chocolate at the cafe

There certainly are good things to be learned from paying close attention to how authors write, so use those favorite books of yours to remind yourself of how you like things described and written about. Even imitating someone else's style you admire is perfectly permissible so long as you are picking out the pieces that sound like you. Those passages that ring true in your own heart. One good practice that can be beneficial to uncovering your own voice is to take notice of and collect quotes and paragraphs that you enjoy. You can easily photocopy these from your reading materials, then cut and paste them right into the pages of your journal. In fact if you read on further you'll see that this book is not just about keeping a <u>written</u> journal of your wonderful stay here on earth, but about doing so through collecting all sorts of things. Be consciously surrounding your being with the words you like. They will slowly submerge themselves into your subconscious

hut in Baja

13

and reemerge one day as your own.

Now these are all dandy suggestions. But what if you find yourself still staring blankly at each new empty page? What if, no matter how hard you try, you still want to rip out about half of those journal pages and gleefully burn each and every one? Once again, don't panic. Remember what our Buddhist friends have to say about these kinds of difficulties: <u>Every problem is an opportunity for learning new things.</u>

And instead of destroying a piece of your work, which one day you may highly value, simply put your journal away for a

Harley in Kentucky

while and go in search of help. Many folks find great inspiration by enrolling in a writing class. This can easily be done in the evening hours after the day's responsibilities are over. Books on how to write are also valuable. Your bookstore should have an entire section devoted to this. I'll list my favorites at the end of this chapter.

Of course there are those rare individuals who, with no apparent training and not a lot of outside influence, can pick up a pen, brush, camera, or stick of old wood and with sleight of hand effortlessly create great works of art. Unfortunately not all of us are that acutely attuned to our creative side naturally, so we'll need to go the route of the laborer, the tinkering artisan, the incoherent dabbler in lofty ideals.

Yes, it is our duty, our everlasting need, to be the ones who go marching

lamppost in Paris

into our unknown futures. We will make that endless journey to the east, fasting until given food, wandering until offered shelter. We, the proud journal makers who cower not at life's sacred offerings, who hardly tremble at destiny's doorway, willingly and with lots of courage, take up our armaments of battle, our pens, notebooks, cameras, and dreams, and plunge headlong and with wreckless abandon into the gathering storms....

(O)ops! You'll have to excuse my outbursts. I do get pretty fanatical when it comes to journal keeping. Hope you are too. Fanaticism can go a long way to bringing you to places you otherwise would never have come. So get on your boots. It's gonna be a long hard climb. And as you're going along, stop lots and learn how to look, listen, and feel again. Like you used to do when you were just a child. Before you got picked up and hurriedly carried into the deluge we call adult- hood.

grain silo in Oregon

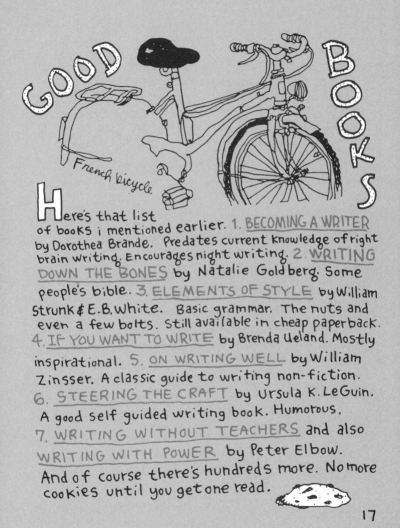

GOOD BOOKS

French bicycle

Here's that list of books i mentioned earlier. 1. <u>BECOMING A WRITER</u> by Dorothea Brande. Predates current knowledge of right brain writing. Encourages night writing. 2. <u>WRITING DOWN THE BONES</u> by Natalie Goldberg. Some people's bible. 3. <u>ELEMENTS OF STYLE</u> by William Strunk & E.B. White. Basic grammar. The nuts and even a few bolts. Still available in cheap paperback. 4. <u>IF YOU WANT TO WRITE</u> by Brenda Ueland. Mostly inspirational. 5. <u>ON WRITING WELL</u> by William Zinsser. A classic guide to writing non-fiction. 6. <u>STEERING THE CRAFT</u> by Ursula K. LeGuin. A good self guided writing book. Humorous. 7. <u>WRITING WITHOUT TEACHERS</u> and also <u>WRITING WITH POWER</u> by Peter Elbow. And of course there's hundreds more. No more cookies until you get one read.

4.
·WONDER ABOUT THINGS·

Shilo holds her pen kinda funny when she draws

Please do bear with me if i seem to be going off the deeper end here in this chapter. As i would like to tell you all about my discoveries with the world of <u>drawing</u>. I was struck so forcefully and passionately by this elemental art form that i totally shelved a 10-year absolute love affair with cameras and photography to follow its primal charms. And it has now completely overtaken my own journal books for the last seven years.

Pitched the tent up in the orchard then realized it was a field full of tiny chickens. Our cousins said that it was okay. That they won't peck holes in it or anything.

You see writing about things is only one way to document them. Sketching is another. And for me it is the ultimate experience. No longer did i need a machine placed between me and reality to do the recording. Forget those stinky darkroom chemicals and expensive films, i would tell my photo friends. All i needed was a little book of pristine white pages and a pocketful of inky pens and i was <u>free</u>. Free to document in whatever way or speed i choose. Instead of hopping out of the car for a quick snapshot, i could pause, sit down, feel the grass, the wind, and meditate upon a beautiful scene. Yes i did say meditate, cause that is exactly what you get to do. Have wonderful meditations and communions with all those things you choose to draw.

That's old Harold on the left and Dave to the right. Just two guys out fishin' on a breezy Saturday morn. "It gets you out of the house," said Dave.

central Utah, heading once again for home

MONTANA

road work

Am i beginning to sound like some sort of nut case? Have you already called to reserve me a room at the Funny Farm? Well fine. I'll happily go there too and draw everything and everyone i see! ⟫⟶ I've become an absolute and total drawing fool. Filled over 30 sketchbooks with meandering lines. Loving every second of it. Seeing no end in sight, even after all these years.

Well, now you know how i feel about the sketching bug. It can grab you when you least expect it and take you places you've never been. So I'd like to propose to all you

20

journal keepers out there, start
doing some <u>drawings</u> around the
corners and down the sides and
make your journals <u>illustrated</u>.

Are those grunts and groans I'm
hearing in the back there?
And the everpresent, "Me? Why i
can't draw a thing." <u>Well let me
tell you something right here
and now</u> Buster. I've not met
even one person in all my travels
that couldn't draw something. One
time i did a photo story on a gal and she didn't
have any arms. And she did beautiful artwork
anyway. You know how? By holding her pens and
brushes between her toes! So i don't want to
hear no baloney about how you can't
draw. Okay?   Okay.

nashville skyline

rabble rousers, Santa Cruz

So here's a little exercise i always do to get people drawing. Because it is true we <u>all</u> really can draw. We just have that old grade school art teacher imprinted on our memories who told us our carefully sketched horse, or whatever we were so proud of, "doesn't look quite right because...." Unfortunately what that teacher failed to recognize and to say is that each one of us has a unique Signature that directly translates to any drawings we make. It's these <u>differences</u> that make our own art interesting. If we had all gone on to be "great" artists with that <u>OLD</u> mentality, then each and everyone

"The sketch hunter has delightful days of drifting about among people, in and out of the city, going anywhere, everywhere, stopping as long as he likes, no need to reach any point, moving in any direction, following the call of interests. He moves through life as he finds it, not passing negligently the things he loves, but stopping to know them, and to note them down in the shorthand of his sketchbook, a box of oils with a few small panels or on his drawing pad. Like any hunter he hits or misses. He is looking for what he loves, he tries to capture it. It is found anywhere, everywhere."

ROBERT HENRI <u>THE ART SPIRIT</u>

of us would be producing "perfect" photo-like sketches. We'd all be <u>NORMAN ROCKWELL</u>. Yikes. Anyway back to the drawing exercise. When I'm at a cafe with someone, i always ask

S A N T A

B A R B A R A

Having breakfast out with Cynthia and Eric and friends Jerry and Lisa. They have a <u>very red</u> sports car

23

them, would they please draw the salt shaker in my journal and then sign their name to it? Well of course this does cause some pretty nervous chatter, but after some cajoling they usually do it.

There are those who simply can't seem to get any kind of line going though, so i talk them thru it, holding up the shaker at different angles and trying to get them to actually <u>look</u> at it. Mostly we don't look at anything for more than a few seconds. Was this something taught us in our childhood? That it's impolite to stare at people and things?

So maybe people should change the idea that they "can't draw", to that they really don't know how to <u>LOOK</u> and how to <u>SEE</u>. If a person can learn to observe clearly, then drawing becomes easy.

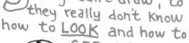

ERIC

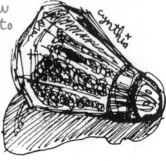

cynthia

Drawing is also a form of meditation and makes you more aware, more living in this present moment. By sitting quietly and looking out onto the world, instead of inward to our old thoughts and desires, we express our wonderment of everything around us. By taking the time to render them with lines on paper, you acknowledge the sacredness of each and every little thing. Even ants and bugs and stuff.

If you think you'd like to include sketches in your journal and want to pursue that great quest to discover your own drawing style, i would suggest you do the same thing mentioned earlier about studying famous authors. Completely immerse yourself in the

in WASHINGTON PARK this fountain makes music from the falling drops

2PM

Kind of books with art that move you. For instance you may be drawn to woodcut or rubber stamp type art. By researching that field you might someday be filling your journal with hand-carved stamps to go with your writing. Or you might be led to water-color painting. Who knows. You may indeed be the next Norman Rockwell or Grandma Moses! These things do happen.

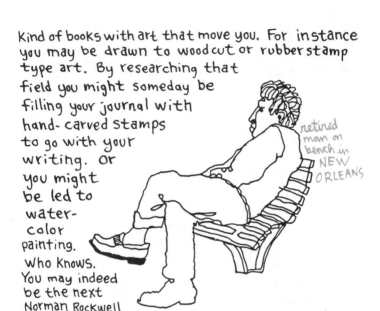

retired man on bench in NEW ORLEANS

"The sketchbook is a private visual diary. In it you are free to study and to learn, to experiment, to splash and paddle around with the ink. It is a record of your own relation-ship to the world, the notes of inner pro-gression. Keep your sketchbook alive. Make it a part of yourself. Each time we open our eyes we create a world which is unique to ourselves. A line is an idea given energy."

ON DRAWING by FRED GETTINGS

So don't forget about the library as being a great place to search. Art stores have all the supplies that can make you crazy deciding which pencil, pen, brush, or paint fits your needs. Equipment is weird. I ended

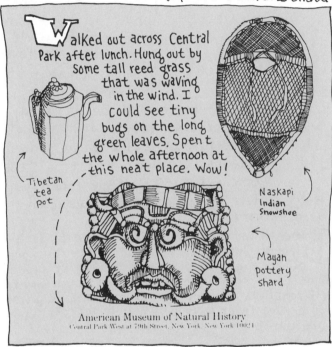

Walked out across Central Park after lunch. Hung out by some tall reed grass that was waving in the wind. I could see tiny buds on the long green leaves. Spent the whole afternoon at this neat place. Wow!

Tibetan tea pot

Naskapi Indian Snowshoe

Mayan pottery shard

American Museum of Natural History
Central Park West at 79th Street, New York, New York 10024

up searching 3 years before i was finally happy with mine.

And while you're there in the library, or the store, or bakery or park, bus station or anywhere, you must remember this. <u>IT'S ALL FAIR GAME</u>! Once you begin to keep a journal, the entire world and everything in it instantly becomes material to be observed, written about, drawn, photographed, or collected in some manner. So don't forget to <u>STOP</u>, <u>LOOK</u>, and <u>LISTEN</u>. And record your days before they get whisked away and soon forgotten.

Some of you may find the courage to do a little journal drawing actually out in public places and not just in the privacy of your own home or backyard or garden. At first you may feel self-conscious doing it, but you'll soon find yourself lost in the reverie of lines and not caring one twit what anyone else thinks.

marys peak is now topped with a layer of snow.

So, are you ready for a quick exercise that frees up your creativity a bit? It's a good way to prove to yourself that you can make unique lines and that you have a left-side logical brain and a creative right side. There's a few popular books you can read that explain this phenomenon. I know i was kinda skeptical about it at first. Anyway what you do is grab a fork or spoon or anything that would be pretty easy to draw, set it there on the kitchen table next to your empty book, and stare at it for about 5 minutes. I know, it's a hard thing to do. Probably the only thing you've ever stared at that long was your computer screen, but stick with it, notice the light, the reflections, your funny face in the curve of the spoon, the contours, and the entire shape of the object.

Okay now, grab your pen or whatever you use, and begin drawing just the very outermost edge

Sheepherder wagons

29

of the object. But here's the catch. <u>YOU CAN-</u>
<u>NOT LOOK AT WHAT YOU'RE DRAWING!</u>
And if you catch yourself peeking, cover
up your journal with a towel or piece of
paper. Just continue to follow that outside edge, slowly and with no worrying.
What's happening now, the reason you're
suddenly all filled with anxiety, is
because that logical part of your brain
is doing the drawing, and when you
cut off its supply of logical inform-
ation, it has baby fits. Cries and
complains. But you must endure. Do
continue on, courageously believing in
your important little lines.

Go right ahead and fill the whole page
with your lines. Then remove the
blind and take a good careful look at all
of them. Go ahead and laugh too. Laugh and
say, well that doesn't look good at all. Just a
bunch of baby scribbles, right? Well look a
little closer. Because if you did continue
with the exercise, and filled the entire page,
then there's a good chance that you
actually forced your left brain to
go away and work on calculus or
something logical, and your right brain

fork

pencil

gleefully took over and began doing what it does best. That is making a direct connection with a thing out there, then creatively rendering it on paper, thru your hand, via the heart. So don't laugh too hard. Because those lines you just drew are pure you, with no "thinking" to confuse the outcome. They may be the purest, most innocent lines you've made since you were a mere toddler. Definitely something new and very valuable. Something that belongs in your journal.

This exercise is old hat and even a daily start-up method for many artists. It's one of the few ways known to get old lefty back doing the dishes, not out dabbling in the fields of creativity. He really isn't so good at that.

I guess the reason that writing and drawing become so darn fun and interesting once you get going on it is because it causes you to take such a

31

different view of the world. Things you once found boring suddenly become filled with possibility. Your wife wants you to drive her down to Wal-Mart? Again?! Well now that you've got a journal you could happily sit in the car and write down all your observations about the varied characters you see coming thru those ever-swinging doors. Or you could make a sketch of one of the cars in the parking lot, or that fat robin on the telephone line.

You see, you've now become an OBSERVER OF LIFE. It's fun. It's exciting. It's way better than going into Wal-Mart and buying more stuff. See, all you need is your book, a

...nature study

...wherein you get yourself right down to the ground to study nature's many bejeweled items. You'll be very amazed looking thru a magnifying glass. Also sit for long times just LOOKING. And you will see all the living things move. Interview a frog, rock. Meditate with a precision rock. Draw with precision and to scale....

Callipepla californica

few inexpensive pens, and you're happy. Like a clam.

Now granted there will be an adjustment period. I myself can vividly remember the sunny day i stopped my car while on a photo assignment, to make a quick sketch of a neat church steeple. When i was all finished i looked at it and said to myself, "Now why in the world did i do that? What does that steeple have to do with me anyway?" Well now i can look back on that and realize what a limited take i had on the world. What does anything out there have to do with you in here? Why would you ever draw some car in the Wal-Mart parking lot? Well because, hopefully, the thing did <u>move</u> you somehow. You were attracted to it for whatever reason. Maybe you parked over here instead of over there because you like old Porsches and here's one you could feast your eyes on. So all these opinions we carry dutifully around with us can in the beginning direct our attention and get us opening our

workers in MEXICO

perception to a bigger world view. If you keep on this path you may become wise and drop the narrow judgements of likes and dislikes and come to realize the beauty in all things. From simple weeds blowing on a windy hill, to the classic curves of old automobiles.

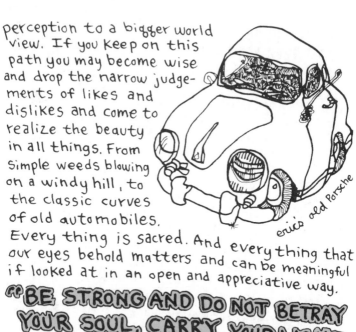

eric's old Porsche

Everything is sacred. And everything that our eyes behold matters and can be meaningful if looked at in an open and appreciative way.

"BE STRONG AND DO NOT BETRAY YOUR SOUL, CARRY YOUR LIGHT TO ILLUMINATE YOUR DESTINY. REJOICE, FOR YOU ARE PART OF THE GREAT MYSTERY."

OLD INDIAN SAYING

34

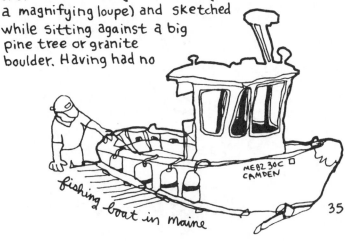

Are you beginning to
see how limitless
the aspects
of keeping a
journal are? When i was first discovering the
magic of journal making i was living in a tipi
in a sunny meadow in Oregon. It was on the
outskirts of a small town and i didn't get
many visitors. To while away the long afternoons
I'd wander up the river with a notebook, pen,
clear tape, and an Exacto knife, collecting all
kinds of interesting specimens. The flat
objects were taped into the journal, then I'd make
notes about where they had been found. Smaller
ones were closely observed (sometimes with
a magnifying loupe) and sketched
while sitting against a big
pine tree or granite
boulder. Having had no

Cabo San Lucas

MEB230C
CAMDEN

fishing boat in Maine

35

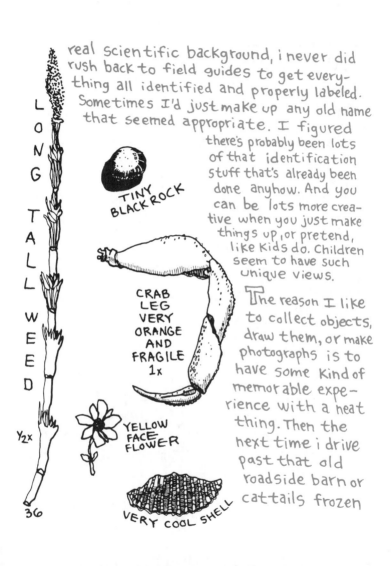

real scientific background, i never did rush back to field guides to get everything all identified and properly labeled. Sometimes I'd just make up any old name that seemed appropriate. I figured there's probably been lots of that identification stuff that's already been done anyhow. And you can be lots more creative when you just make things up, or pretend, like kids do. Children seem to have such unique views.

The reason I like to collect objects, draw them, or make photographs is to have some kind of memorable experience with a neat thing. Then the next time i drive past that old roadside barn or cattails frozen

LONG TALL WEED

½x

36

TINY BLACK ROCK

CRAB LEG VERY ORANGE AND FRAGILE 1x

YELLOW FACE FLOWER

VERY COOL SHELL

in the snow, i can remember back and say "Oh yah. Hi. How ya doin? I remember you. I stopped to admire and sketch you 2 years ago, on that long past summer morning." This way i am creating actual, real, and intimate relationships with many things out there in our world. And it has been the most meaningful and fulfilling thing I've ever done.

I feel closer and more connected to my own two children since documenting their lives. One day i know they will look back over all this scribbling and be very thankful and appreciative. That thankyou letter i anticipate getting way out there in the future makes all the work worthwhile today.

corn

6 years old ANNA the neighbor girl.

Chick foot

H_2O

NEW BABY CHICKS AT MY SISTER'S HOUSE

feathers

Heater

37

a walk with shilo

First of all we walked real slow, saying hello to neighbors and looking at the animals in the fields. Pretty soon Shilo wanted to draw a cow so she sat down next to a white gate and started making lines. Normally I'd stare close at her lines as they came out of her pen, cause thats my favorite thing to do, but suddenly i was struck by the scene of all that long pasture grass waving in the wind.....

I looked real hard at one barn so i could draw it when we got home.

Shilo counted 14 horses...

we saw one bird...

Mostly we just walked along and thot our own thots.

we crossed many bridges.

Shilo wondered about things. Like why was that tall fence there and whats it like inside that old abandoned house.

I worried that maybe a fast car would come to smash us off the road and into a dirty ditch, and would our spirits fly off and up to the OTHER WORLD? And also i thot that maybe most all my thoughts are just fluff from a dandelion blowin in the wind. That maybe it would be better to just not think.

Shilo said she wanted to "fix up" her cow drawing when we got home but I'm just gonna glue it in here right now.

thats one horsetail plant we found by a stream.

COW by SHILO ROSE

38

D. PRICE 1996

It would be real easy to go on and on here, but maybe the best thing is to just let you make the endless discoveries that await the enthusiastic journal keeper. I remember once staying overnight in the studio of California artist Earl Thollander, who has kept an amazing travel sketch journal for the last 50 years. Entire shelves are filled with journals that document his amazing life all around the world. Now Earl hosts other artists on junkets to far-flung ports of call and continues to enjoy keeping visual records of his varied days. We should all be so lucky. We should all make our own lives a work of art.

—Earl Thollander

39

5.

•LESS IS MORE•

You probably won't find a chapter on photography in most books on how to keep a diary. But because cameras are so widely used these days, it makes sense to utilize all that energy into something meaningful and worthwhile. Remember how your mother always used to say, ".'.Someday I'll get all those pictures sorted out and into photo albums." But somehow or for whatever reason it just never got done. Mainly because of  the sheer size of the task. And what's really scary is that many of our mothers are still taking more pictures! Yikes.

Just think about it. There you go off on your summer vacation with that everpresent camera and several rolls of film. And sooner or later the darn thing ends up around your neck with you straining to capture all the neat moments. That special lunch in the park. Kids poking sleepy heads out of dewy tents. Frolics on the beach (so that's where that sand came from). The group shot in front of the museum, wienie roasts, and on and on and on.

One day the kids and i found one of those
old-fashioned photo booths. The pictures were
edited, trimmed, and then glued in our journal.

41

Then a few weeks later you pick up your pictures and everyone passes them around the dinner table. People laugh, people smile. Maybe one or two get set aside and end up behind a magnet on the refrigerator. And the rest, well they usually end up in "the box." That amazingly interesting but definitely intimidating box in the closet that is spilling over with all those frozen moments.

Because most people don't know what to do with all these leftovers (you say your photo albums are all finished and up to date? Amazing. You get 2 more cookies), they usually stay in the box, lost to the light of day, forgotten.

But do not despair, surely there must be a way to successfully incorporate the better ones

42

to a higher status. If you're willing to plan ahead and maybe do a little photographic study. Sound interesting?

First of all, let's hope all you journal keepers will be taking your empty books on all your neat excursions. This will benefit you in two ways. First you'll be slowing down and spending some time writing and drawing your experiences, which is way better than snapping at them with a camera. And second, all that calmness will cause you to be making <u>fewer</u> pictures. Yea! Fewer being the key word here. And instead of putting them in "the dreaded picture box" after your fun trip, i propose that you include your most favorite ones right in your journal. It's real easy. Here's how.

"The photographer collects things with his eye. The secret of photography is that the camera takes on the character and the personality of the handler. The mind works on the machine."

Walker Evans THE HUNGRY EYE

As you're writing along, remember to leave some pages empty here and there, then return at a later date to fill them in with pictures. There are three words that you need to know here that could help you to make a more interesting journal. And they are edit, edit, and edit. Why is it that we treat our snapshots like sacred objects? I know several people who refuse to throw away even the all-black prints. And they get double prints! Yikes. I shot several rolls of film, everyday, for ten years, and believe me lots of them were duds. So don't be afraid to cull, to edit, to throw about half of them away even. Burn them. It's great fun to stand by the burn barrel and watch them crinkle and melt.

So be a good editor and keep only the best shots. If you could do this, you would already have half your photography battle won. If you already do this, congratulations. Have some more cookies. ☺

Now don't let me hurt your feelings, but it probably needs to be said. Most of us don't have the eyes of van Gogh, so you can bet that many of your shots may be poorly composed. My own mom was famous for getting lots and lots of sky and clouds with little rows of cutoff heads down at the bottom. And pictures of thumbs?

45

We had hundreds. Unfortunately it's a little bit difficult to go back and retake the pictures, so you'll have to utilize some old tricks of the newspaper business: scissors and cropping.

Yes, you too can become one of those green-visored editors and cut out all (well most) of that blue sky above Aunt Maude. And you say you just love that shot of your new car except for your pesky neighbor's head spying from behind the picket fence? Snip. Snip. No more neighbor. My kids and i have even gone so far as to dump a bunch of pictures on the floor, then begin tearing off corners and excessive areas, unwanted things and people, until we have a new pile of rough-edged photographs that are then glued down into collages in our journals and captioned.

So, as you can see, the possibilities, just like with writing and drawing, are simply endless. All you gotta do is get <u>CREATIVE</u>. Photographs, when glued, taped, or fastened with old-time photo corners, can add immeasurably to your journals power to <u>REMIND.</u> And it just doesn't have to be vacation pictures either. Some people spend their lives studying different things of interest, highlighting their notes

with photographs.

Now here's one of those neat moments that only a camera can capture. I had been on a half-day hike with my wife

back in the old days. We had us a white 1963 Volkswagen bug and because the weather was so nice she sat in the window as i slowly made our way through the woods and back out to the highway.

It can be fun to experiment. These pictures were taken with a half-frame Olympus camera, which puts two images in one 35mm rectangle.

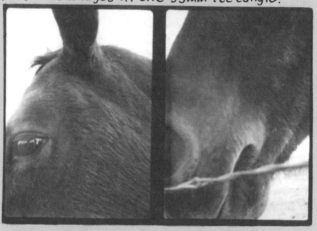

"Whether artist or not, the photographer is a joyous sensualist, for the simple reason that the eye traffics in feelings, not in thoughts. The photographer is in effect a voyeur by nature, but also reporter, tinkerer, and spy. What keeps him going is pure absorption, incurable childishness." Walker Evans THE HUNGRY EYE

Don't forget to try out one of those pens that will write on photographs. You can draw arrows to identify people and places and make the photographs more personalized. Black out your best friend's teeth! Draw little stubby horns on that mother-in-law. But most of all have **FUN**! The fun you get out of creating this big, thick scrapbook of your life will be automatically translated to you or whoever picks it up and reads it in the future.

So, now that I have hopefully convinced you that keeping your best snapshots in your journal is a possibility, why don't we give you some good pointers on making better photographs than the ones you've made in the past? Like i said before, i took tons of photographs while working as a newspaper photographer for all those years and i sort of came up with the four most important things that make a good photograph. They're even kind of a secret, so you have to promise you'll only tell your closest friends. And maybe your mother, if you think it would help. My mom takes pretty good pictures these days.

Okay here they are. The four rules that if followed rather closely will pretty much insure a good picture. 1. PICK A GOOD SUBJECT. Now you gotta think about this one. Is that

49

deer way out in the field going to even show up? And all your friends know how much you like close-up pictures of flowers, but do they need to see another package of prints of even more flowers? Picking your photographic subject isn't like picking your nose. Not just any old booger will do. You must try to come up with subject matter that is not only interesting but that can be successfully photographed as well.

Children are a good place to start. They soon forget you are even around which helps to get unposed "everybody smile now and act like you're having a great time" type pictures. Or instead of the old traditional "here we are at the...." kind of snapshots, try to be creative and photograph things you've never photographed before. I have a friend in New York who took a picture of every significant door in his partner's life, made it into a little reminiscent type booklet, and presented it to

One day i took an entire 36 exp. roll of my boy picking his nose. I have a contact sheet of it somewhere. It's pretty funny. After that, whenever we saw him picking his nose we'd point and say "Nose-picker! Nosepicker."

her as a gift. I did a similar thing with all my favorite pictures of my wife and made her a book that is still fun to look thru as we grow older.

So make sure you have a good subject you're staring at thru the lens.

Rule number 2. <u>GET TO KNOW YOUR CAMERA IN AN INTIMATE WAY</u>. You could become so familiar with its many knobs, buttons, switches, and lenses that making pictures becomes totally automatic to you. Or try this. Sit down and <u>DRAW</u> your camera. It's a great way to get yourself to really look closely at it. You can handle and use your camera daily and make it an extension of your arm and thoughts. This is essential in order to know what it will and won't do. Bulk loading your own film is a much cheaper alternative that

NEW SUNGLASSES

(ask your photo-store guy)

enables you to shoot more film. Shooting pictures is just like anything else, the more you do
it the better you will get. And how many times
have you seen someone fumbling and fighting
with the mechanical controls of their battery-
dead camera? Myself i prefer the old-style man-
ual cameras because they can be adjusted to make
different kinds of pictures without some invisible-
automatic-super-computer-chip between the shooter
and the subject, making decisions on its own.

So take your camera everywhere with you for an
extended period of time and learn to capture
those little gems in life that move you. Then

by sheer repetition you'll find yourself antic-
ipating those up-and-coming moments and be
able to get them on film. All because your little
picture maker has truly become part of your
life and not something you keep forgetting back
home in the drawer. That black box with its
magical glass eye is the perfect companion for
gathering up the scattered bits and pieces of
a life.

☐ 'll tell you the third secret rule in a minute.
First i want to show you this picture of my
daughter Shilo Rose. She was up in her monkey
tree where she used to hide. I took it with one of
those tiny Minox spy cameras. It takes shots up close.

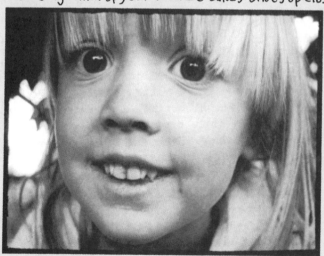

Okay I'm back. It's so easy to get diverted while trying to get this book written, by my own diary. Just spent the weekend snowboarding with the kids and took my little empty book along to sketch the skiers. And last night i also took it along to write by the fire at a snow camp about a half mile up river from my place. How wonderfully satisfying it is to write down those late-night thoughts and revelations, to draw sticks and pinecones and tents and tipis, then walk back to the studio the next day and paint some of them with watercolors under the morning sun.

So back we go to all this picture business. Rule number ③ is <u>LEARN WHAT GOOD COMPOSITION IS</u> and think about what you are seeing thru the camera before pushing the shutter release. The main reason people don't like their own photographs when they come back from the developer is because their eyes saw one thing and the camera another. Standing at the edge of the Grand Canyon is an awesome experience, but don't expect your Instamatic with its narrow 50mm lense to see and capture what you do.

my home

54

Shilo was so small when she was a baby that she fit in a garden water bucket.

Now granted that word "composition" is a bit of a tricky one. When you shorten it a little you have compose, which means to construct. Or maybe arrange would be a better word. Because there's no doubt about it with a camera, what you see in that rectangle is probably what you're going to get.

So don't rush yourself. Try lots of different views, levels, and angles before taking the picture. Is your subject more of a vertical nature than horizontal? Well then turn your camera sideways and shoot it long and tall. Do you want to fill the entire frame with faces like above? Then move in closer. And

don't worry, people don't generally bite. Dogs
do though, sometimes when you least expect
it. I think a good and probably general rule
is to <u>COMPOSE</u> your shot, then take <u>TWO</u> large
steps forward. The idea being that you want
to do as much cropping in the viewfinder as
possible, so as to keep your pictures more
immediate and strong. It also helps to move
around so that your background is clean and
simple. We don't need light poles growing out
of grandma's head or a whole field of grass
with you pointing to the speck saying, "See
that pheasant? Oh man, you should have
seen it. She was a real beauty." Once again

there are lots of art and photography books that can teach you what the words "good composition" mean. But in the end you'll have to devise your own ideas, designs, and outcomes that will make them your photos and not just a copied idea from something you read about or saw.

One surefire way to do this is through an exercise i call the Art of Glancing. We all glance here and there during our lifetimes, each seeing special little moments and locking them in our minds. After you have become quite handy with your camera and feel that you can use it quickly and without much thought, go out and buy some cheap, on-sale film, load up and shoot several rolls <u>without looking</u> <u>through the lens</u>!

Now your left brain will be having sissy fits, just like with that drawing exercise. But try it anyway. Whenever you see something you think would make a neat picture, examine it some, then SNAP. Take a photograph of it without any further

on the upper deck at the Kentucky Derby

Kentucky tobacco barn

thought. And when the pictures come back you may be pleasantly surprised. You will have been making pictures with your very creative right-side brain and they will be fresh and new and vibrant.

At this point I need to offer you a warning. For this is that unchartered territory for some that can lead to addiction. In dabbling in these creative voids you may peer into that vast chasm called Art. (Oh my goodness.... he said the A word.) Once you feel its powerful pull (it's a quite magnificent feeling actually), Shhhh! Once you are drawn in, your eyes may become glassy and you won't be able to wait to get off work so you can run home and create, create, create. You get the picture?

So do be careful. Once the ole creative juices get flowing you might just find yourself off on some wild picture hunt. Like some crazy spy in the bushes with your little glass eye......it happened to me.   61

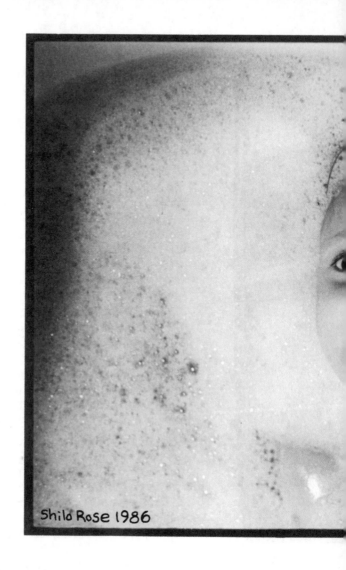

Shilo Rose 1986

Well you're wondering about that final fourth rule I'll bet. Well I'm gonna keep you wondering while i write right over the top of this kid picture. It's of that darn Shilo who wouldn't get out of the tub one night. So what did i do? I got creative and made her picture. And now I'm getting creative again and <u>writing</u> on the white space instead of to one side. So when you choose to be creative, things always work out. Shilo eventually did get out of that tub (I think) and now you get to see her funny picture in a book. So have some fun in your life, dang it.

Rule number four is: <u>LEARN TO WAIT FOR A REALLY GOOD MOMENT.</u> Instead of wildly snapping at any old thing that moves, try to distill your vision somewhat. Be a quiet, alert witness to all those events going on around you. And when you catch a glimpse of that certain smile or neat →

gesture, SEIZE the MOMENT. Now this will take some practice. But if you position yourself more as a "fly on the wall" instead of "Hi I'm here to take pictures", you will not only get better shots but also maybe learn how to actually <u>see</u> better, which in turn can make you <u>feel</u> better, and just, well, <u>everything</u> can become much better in your life. Are you starting to see how this all works?

1988

SORGHUM MAKER

"Hey Shane. How many pages have i done on the photography part?" Shane's my son. We like to give him math problems. "24 pages Dad." Well that ought to be enough. I think you got all my ideas. Try some out. No cookies till you do.

"Believe in yourself. Believe in your capacity. Believe in your goodness. Seek adventure. Climb high mountains. Run wild rivers. Live daily with this spirit. Take care. Follow your dreams, but watch your step. Have fun, sing, dance, laugh, and spread joy wherever you journey."

ROYAL ROBBINS

6.
· STUDY REALITY ·

Okay put that camera down for awhile and read on here about how to become a Naturalist and make forays into the wild to collect cool specimens for your journal. There's an endless variety of interesting things growing all around you and there isn't any reason why you couldn't include some of it right along with your photos, drawings, paintings, and writing. For some folks putting all these things together might be a bit much for their one empty book. If that's the case then feel free to keep one or more items separate. You may want to have one book for plants only.

Out there in the natural world are all sorts of sticks, leaves, flowers, seeds, grasses, and butterfly wings. Things way down there below our field of vision. Things we walk on and hardly ever take notice of.

"I wish I could paint without me existing. That just my hands were there. I wish I could be a Rattler going through these woods, looking up at the branches in the sunlight, the leaves falling down on top of me. When I'm alone in the woods, across these fields, I forget all about myself. I don't exist."

from THE ART OF ANDREW WYETH

MOMS
FLOWERS
DADS
WHITE
PINE

9.94

CONDON, OREGON

near the shoe
string cafe in
september '94.

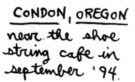

9.7.94
one of
the first
red leaves
found near
Shiba bike
rack on her 1st day
of school.

baby clovers
found under
the car door.
9.10

68

A few years back i was heading down some old lonely road, looking for things of interest to draw, when i dropped my pen and got down in the leaves to look for it. And right away i was struck with how many tiny plants and bugs and pieces of nature were there just out of sight. So that's when i started carrying a small magnifying glass and collecting lots of flat objects in the journal.

razor knife

magnifying glass

I say flat because unless you want a big, thick, and bulky book, you better collect only those items that are pretty flat to begin with. Instead of taping an entire pinecone onto a page, why not just a few of its seeds? And i know a lot of people use an actual plant press, but i opted to just flatten and dry flowers in the back pages of the journal, then tape them in at a later date. The taping method i use was taught to us by an old-time plant collector who made book markers and letterhead stationery out of her collected pieces. Only a few of the flowers have lost their color over the years in our journals. Because we tend to collect non-fading plants, this quick taping-down method seems to work.

roll of crystal clear tape

tweezers

plant press (optional)

cookies

So now when I'm out traveling around, i usually have the tools there on the previous page, in my knapsack. When i notice a nice flower or interesting stem of grass i whip out the trusty roll of <u>clear</u> tape, pull some out with the sticky side up (sometimes it gets all criss-crossed and ends up in a ball), and lay the flower on the tape with the prettiest side down. Then you can carefully trim off any excess, unneeded tape and prudently press it onto a journal page. Most flowers do fine being pressed in this manner if you remember to poke a tiny hole or two thru the tape. This aids in the proper drying of the plant and keeps it from rotting or getting moldy.

Now i don't have to tell you scientific types what to do next, as you more than likely already have your field guides out. And if identifying plants and flowers is your cup of tea, then pour away. Some people fill entire pages of their notebooks in this manner and make a strong connection to nature by doing so. The main thing to remember about the rules to journal making, are that there aren't any. Rules, that is. And maybe we could all learn from nature, to take

nat'u·ral·ist, *n.*   One versed in natural sciences, as a botanist.—

time out from all our running about and living and looking up and out and ahead. To just sit quietly looking <u>DOWN</u>. Gathering dandelions in a breezy meadow, or lying on your back in the sunshine, may be the most memorable thing you end up doing all week. The more special you can make these moments and in turn your life, the more there'll be to document.

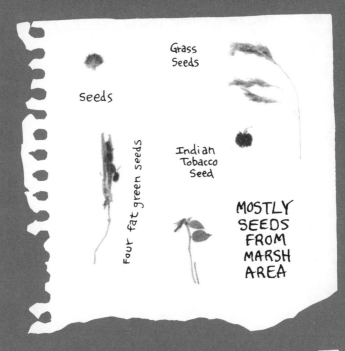

Seeds

Grass Seeds

Four fat green seeds

Indian Tobacco Seed

MOSTLY SEEDS FROM MARSH AREA

"**F**ar away there in the sunshine are my highest aspirations. I may not reach them, but i can look up and see their beauty, believe in them and try to follow where they lead."

LOUISA
MAY
ALCOTT

7.
THE BEST STUFF IN LIFE IS FREE

Are you a collector? Seems like most of the good journal keepers are. They have a passion for noticing and gathering all those things of value to them. Collectors of life, you might say. Hopefully you are a collector also. You will find this activity to be very calming. Small details that you once passed over may come into full view. Things you usually took for granted can become tools to evoke memory. The most insignificant things, vastly important.

If you truly did enjoy seeing that movie at the cinema last night, then maybe you could glue the ticket stub in your journal and write about why you liked it. One of the saddest sights in the world is seeing all those discarded Christmas trees so soon after the holidaze. »——→

hand-carved stamps by Anna Johnson

And when you think about it, we do that same thing with all kinds of objects. What an interesting assortment of items we'd have if we began to save them and use them as little decorations in our diaries.

At my sister's farmhouse, right there above the sink, are stuck layer upon layer of colorful fruit stickers. A sort of ongoing work of art really. And a good example of turning what may be an annoyance into a positive thing.

When you decide to look at the world in this new way, then life becomes an adventure, because you are always on a treasure hunt, saving things like that little piece of paper on the end of your tea bag. The one with the good quote on it. Or the wrapper on your favorite candy bar, or the label on that special bottle of wine. Cigar wrappers, foreign or old stamps, business cards, hotel letterhead, rubber stamps, little found articles, funny cartoons, the logo from the sack of your favorite store, the window sticker on your new car!

POSTMARKS

These are a little hard to get, but if you ask very politely, show the postal clerk a sheet with several others, and say it's for your stamp collection, you'll usually get it. I'll bet most postal workers were stamp collectors when they were kids.

* Only in Houston and Palm Springs did they say no when I asked.

↑ all National Parks now have these cool "Passport" stamps at their visitor centers.

SANTA FE, NM
NOV
3
1995
USPS

SANTA BARBARA, CALIF.
NOV
22
1994
MILPAS STA.

IDAHO 83340-9998 KETCHUM
JAN
24
1996

NEW ORLEANS, LA VIEUX CARRE STA.
OCT
23
1995
USPS

BIG SUR, CA
FEB
16
1996
USPO

Little Bighorn Battlefield Nat'l Mon.
OCT 20 '96
Crow Agency, Mont.

SEAL COVE, ME
AUG
13
A 4
1996
04674

PARKSVILLE
OCT
28
1999
KY
USPO

BILOXI, MS M.O.
OCT
30
1996
USPS

EVEN
ODDBALL
STUFF

SHANE'S

DAD'S

SHILO'S, see how it forms an 'S'?

↑ one day we blew up our own fingerprints on a copy machine

CHÈVRE des TERRES JAUNES 45 % MG mini BAUDUEN MAREC 94 70 09 59

cheese sticker

NICOLAS POUSSIN 1594-1665 peintre et le film de Andro 440 LA POSTE 1994 RÉPUBLIQUE FRANÇAISE BOUCHES 13-11

a foreign postmark

rubber stamp

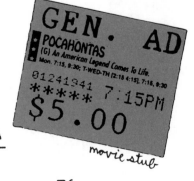

GEN. AD
POCAHONTAS
(G) An American Legend Comes To Life.
Mon. 7:15, 9:30; T-WED-TH (2:15 4:15); 7:15, 9:30
01241941
***** 7:15PM
$5.00

movie stub

Any actual physical artifacts from your voyage thru life will do, from favorite old letters to last week's airline ticket stub. Just remember that like all those things out in nature you've been hauling home, only keep the flat ones, or your book will begin to re-semble an overstuffed piece of luggage.

BE FREE

Of course now you're beginning to get imaginings of just how endlessly fun this all could be. Like a kid in a candy store, don't be surprised to find yourself haunting rubber stamp stores or watching the sidewalks for a rare treasure. I know one lady who even keeps the tags off her favorite clothes when they get thread-bare. My boy Shane even taped in a piece of his already chewed bubblegum to a journal page on a trip to Baja last year. Strange boy.

GET
RUBBER
STAMP
MADNESS!

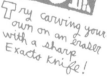

Try carving your own on an eraser with a sharp Exacto knife!

8.

GO FIND YOUR BLISS

I was thinking that a chapter on finding the perfect empty book might be of help to you. Most bookstores now carry a wide assortment of them, and it's a little confusing to decide. Big or little? Spiral or hard bound? Lines or no lines? Gaudy or plain? Quotes on each page or entirely empty? Jees, it's enough to make you just not get one at all.

You can, however, wade into this sea of empty books with a few pointers from folks who have been using them for years. Master journalist Hannah Hinchman says to avoid those supposed empty journals that are already filled with someone else's ideas of good quotes. The whole point being that it's _your_ book and only you can decide what is worthy of going in. New York diarist Daniel Gregory says to at all costs avoid those cumbersome, heavy, hardbound books that are like trying to open an alligator's jaws. The biggest problem with them is trying to get the darn things to stay open and flat, so that you can actually do some work in them. Surely whoever designed those books never tried to use them.

And what about size? Well I'll never forget one of my own journals that ended up getting only half filled because it was so big and heavy. I used to carry it on wilderness trips in my backpack until i realized it was the heaviest item i was packing. So although i dearly loved that old leather-bound law book, i eventually downsized. And who wants to pull out some big, burdensome, noticeable note-book when your aim may be to cultivate a more quiet, discreet, witnessing kind of experience?

Some journal keepers and most artists like to carry pocketsize booklets in order to quickly capture those fleeting visions, take notes on color, or sketch that character in the corner. Upon returning home or to the studio, they can then transfer these ideas onto larger, more permanent, ongoing projects such as paintings, books, and journals.

fancy chair
in PARIS

So what all this really boils down to is what do YOU like? What is your own style of documentation? Maybe right now you don't know. Maybe each and every year it will change, change is good. That's what makes it all so interesting. You may want some huge honkin' scrapbook to collect flowers in. You may want to do drawings and paintings in a teenie-weenie sketchbook like the miniaturists do. You may want to keep your thoughts on banana leaves! who knows? who cares? You're only doing this for one person and that is yourself. No big board of directors or art critics here. So stretch out and dream what you would like to use. And if you still don't find what you're looking for after that fourth rack of empty books, join the club. Most of us are so darn picky there's only one route

GALLO

left to take. <u>WE MAKE OUR OWN BOOKS!</u> (Yikes. Did he say make your own book? How in the world do you do that?) Easy Bozo Nose. Unlike most everything else that's ready-made for us in these modern days of our world, your own journal book is something

you could ably even on your own. and probably Should make

☐ f you continue on this quest in earnest you will find yourself returning yet again and even again to face that big Scary labyrinth known as "the empty book aisle". (Kettle drum Sounds in background.) Since you will eventually fill literally

1.

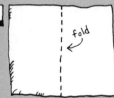

fold

Get real feely and go on a day long paper search. Touch them, rub them, caress each and every edge. Then purchase a ream of your favorite kind, go home and begin to fold it to a size you love. Then treat your yourself to more of those cookies. This is not easy work.

2.

You may need to use a large clip or a big pile of books to get it to stay folded. Be easy on it as paper has feelings too you know. It will usually do what you want without too much hassle.

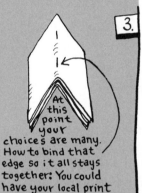

At this point your choices are many. How to bind that edge so it all stays together: You could have your local print shop or Kinko's do a saddle stitch with big staples. 3 is better than 2.

fun part →

Or you could pound nails all along the spine, then sew together with good old dental floss (use mint, it smells better). Or you could use an actual bookmaker's awl and real thread. These bookmakers babies work great.

BOARD

3. hundreds of books with your scrawling scribblets, wouldn't it make sense to personalize the whole process one more step by making your own? Many people are now doing this very thing. Some going so far out in left field as to be making their own paper. Woooooooow.

On these pages are a few ideas on how to proceed. Remember too that you could always take a bookbinding class. Ah yes, bookmaking, one of those almost forgotten crafts from the old world.

You may be asking, but what about the cover? Well i guess you can get as overly complicated as you want to on this one. Personally i like to go ahead and just work on, and live with the

83

new book for awhile.
And then without any
warning a neat piece
of heavy paper will
show up and say "Hey
you, journal writer
guy. Why not use me

for your cover?" So then i take that paper home,
cut it so it overhangs the edges of the book just
a tad bit, then glue it onto the first and last
pages. Then to secure it further and
make the book stronger, i cover the
whole thing with a layer of
that clear packing tape. This way you can
still see the cover paper you found and not
have it get torn or ruined when you set it on
a wet or abrasive surface. ☺

So that's just about all i know about keeping a
journal. I do hope these ideas inspire you to
begin collecting all the meaningful fragments of
your life into some sort of coherent whole.

Of course there will be days when life's busy ways
will keep you seemingly light-years away from

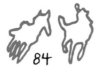

84

your journal. But that only makes you appreciate your sacred time with it all the more.

Of all the many things I've done in my lifetime, I'd have to say that the journals and sketchbooks hold the most meaning. In them are so many important memories that i can easily return to. Simply by pulling one off the studio shelf and climbing in a big comfortable chair, I'm transported to a time long ago through stories, drawings, photographs, and bits of nature.

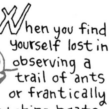

When you find yourself lost in observing a trail of ants or frantically sketching boats

moving in and out of some sunny harbor, you'll realize you've arrived and will smile. You have trained yourself to be a chronicler of life and your long days will be filled with wonder.

HAPPY JOURNALING!

d.price

85

Shilos
YOGURT CHOCOLATE CHIP COOKIE RECIPE

- ½ cup sugar
- ½ cup b. sugar
- ¼ cup butter
- ¼ cup shortening
- ½ cup plain yogurt
- 1½ tsp almond extract
- 1¾ cup flour
- ½ tsp b. soda
- ½ tsp salt
- 1 cup chocolate chips, um, umm.

Okay, here we go. First you gotta turn the oven to 375°. Then beat up all the sugars and butter and shortening and YOGURT and almond stuff, says Shilo. Shane says to mix in 4 Moon Pies, but don't do that. Then mix in the flour, soda, and salt, and mix it up man, mix it up! Whew! Don't forget the CHOCOLATE. Use the whole darn bag if you want. Bake for 8-10 minutes then down the ole pie hole they go! And heed my warning. You may become addicted!

eat me!

eat me now!

86

The following 20 pages are excerpts from my own journal that was published between 1991 and 1998 as a magazine called the →

MOONLIGHT CHRONICLES

NOTE: All misspellings in my journal are on purpose, just becuzz.. 87

— FALLEN DOWN BARN — 1991

About the first 10 issues where all pretty bad as i was learning how to draw and write down my experiences. Enthusiasm is something I've never been short on though, so i plugged away daily, trying different pens and papers and working to render all the neat things i was encountering. In the end it was my daughter's odd way of saying things that taught me to write, and my boy's strange sketching style that taught me to draw.

COUGAR

SHANE BOY has a neat AUDUBON calendar in his bedroom. Lots of good animal photos to draw from. Today is Feb. 16TH and I have come to Corvallis.

88

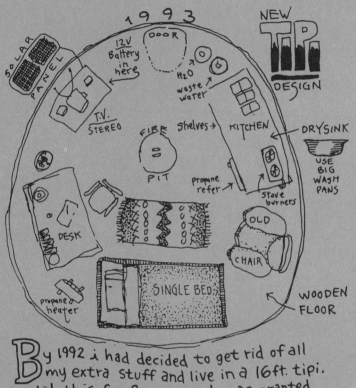

1 9 9 3

NEW TiPi DESIGN

SOLAR PANEL

12V Battery in here

DOOR

H₂O

waste water

KITCHEN

DRYSINK

USE BIG WASH PANS

T.V. STEREO

FIRE PIT

shelves →

propane refer →

stove burners

DESK

OLD CHAIR

propane heater

SINGLE BED

WOODEN FLOOR

By 1992 i had decided to get rid of all my extra stuff and live in a 16ft. tipi. I did this for 3 years and was granted plenty of time to work on the 75 page journals. About 6 issues a year were printed at Kinkos and sent out to 100 subscribers.

WHIPTAIL

2X

As the years passed all the studying and searching began to pay off. I began to see a style emerge and started relaxing and following the natural path of my interests. Some days the kids and i became Naturalists, other days we were watercolor artists.

a few years ago a friend from Kentucky sent this beautiful brass cook stove for Christmas. Just right for making tea and hot meals while on a long WALK....

1994

SVEA

90

At one point i became so addicted to journal making that i sold my car and began doing long hoboesque treks. Here's a page from a 15 day adventure on foot and hitchhiking across Oregon.

↓

road killed bird - 8 miles north of CECIL

- walked 13 miles in SCALDING sun to Ione. Nothin out here but sagebrush, noisy crows and BAD water. Walked to Lexington. Make rash move and hitch all the way into PENDLETON town with wild Catholic-37-year-old-rodeo-queen-bad-drivin-fast-talkin-GAL from Hepner. All these crazy people. what a life... not knowing where you might sleep come the sundowns.

3PM

91

Simple

After walking across Oregon, my journaling life took an unexpected and quite extraordinary turn. I had requested a pair of shoes for the Oregon trip from the very young but rapidly growing <u>Simple</u> shoe company. I slipped an issue of the <u>Chronicles</u> in a letter to the company's owner Eric Meyer.

Several months later Meyer called me and said he wanted to talk about the possibility of merging the <u>Chronicles</u> with their shoe catalog and sending it out to people everywhere.

<u>wow</u>! okay!

Within a matter of weeks my vagobond life was transformed. I bought a new set of clothes and a new car and began monthly forays to the shoe company's headquarters in Santa Barbara. I helped design ads and drew funny pictures for the shoe boxes. But mostly i had been given a 4-year-contract and salary to

1993

GO. NOW.
OKAY.

simple

ERIC AT THE TERMINAL OF THOT.

wander about and create a 168 page travel journal. I was told to go find the secret to life and write about it. Basically it was a total dream job and for the next 4 years i got to see and draw and photograph and write about the endless wonders of this world we live on.

the New MUSEUM of MODERN ART bldg. in downtown San Francisco. No time to go in today.

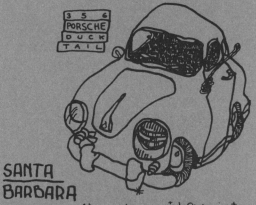

356
PORSCHE
DUCK
TAIL

SANTA BARBARA

You know traveling can be so weird. One minute your over here and the next your way, way over there. Coming over the winding coast mountains i saw an old guy pushing along a loaded down bike. And all the way into SANTA BARBARA i was thinking jees, here I am already <u>here</u>, and yet that fellow on the bike won't cross over for 2 or even maybe 3 days. For some reason i just couldn't ~~stop~~ thinkin about that.... now I'm at Eric and Cynthia's house. They're the ones who own Simple.

1956
BUICK
SPECIAL

95

PARIS · OBSERVATOIRE · (14e) · BD MONTPAR. 12 h 7 -1 1995

BONAFORET

la Ronde des Pains

PARIS

This was a very good day.
Did some walking around
with the roomates after
a breakfast of bread & fruit.
Mailed off letters. Visited
NOTRE-DAME. Looked real
hard at all the angels and
saints and devils. They're
all over that place.

Jennifer
Gallegos

96

Jill Ann
DeJuce

Awoke next morning to the sound of snowflakes falling on the tent. About 4 inches on the ground so i packed up and drove on before sunrise. Down a

CHACO CULTURE NATIONAL HISTORICAL PARK
NOV 04 '95
BLOOMFIELD, N. MEX.

HUNGO PAVI · 900-1100 AD · UNEXCAVATED

long rough road into CHACO. Way to cold for any significant drawing. Found this pot shard. Looked hard at all the intricate work watched the visitor center video. The Anasazi lived her 1000 years ago then mysteriously left. No one knows why.

rock and the

1×

97

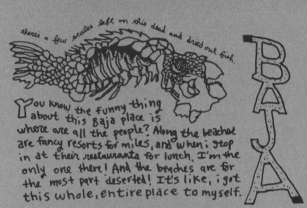

there's a few scales left on this dead and dried out fish.

BAJA

You know the funny thing about this Baja place is where are all the people? Along the beaches are fancy resorts for miles, and when i stop in at their restaurants for lunch, I'm the only one there! And the beaches are for the most part deserted! It's like, i got this whole, entire place to myself.

CAMPSITE
NUMBER 3

BAJA
BEE

1x

MARIANA

the ADRIANA and MARIANA dry docked on the cove area next to tonights campsite.

Shane and i were walking along the beach today when he spotted this little bird thats legs were all tangled up in string. So we got him out and ran to show the girls. He was very alert and would bite your finger with his strong beak. Then we let him go. He flew to a nearby bush and chirped.

Noon has come. We are still on the beach. A never ending roar comes from the ocean. Shane and Shilo are on the water's edge, lassoing waves with long whip-like seaweed. The other game they play is to spin round and round in the tidal zone, then run dizzily towards the beach, just as small waves nip at their feet. Now Shilo is jump roping the seaweed string. Shane is digging holes with his toes and letting each incoming wave bury him deeper and deeper. It is Monday and we have miles of open beach all to ourselves. Just us, a few seagulls and foggy mists rising off the water.

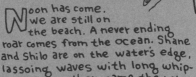

OREGON coast

99

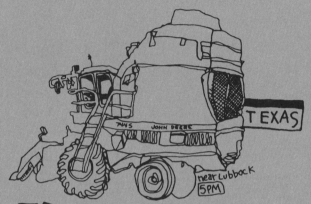

near Lubbock
5PM

You may already know this, but i didn't. Texas grows a lot of **COTTON** and this John Deere is one of the machines used to get it picked. Didn't see anyone doing it by hand, like in the olden days.

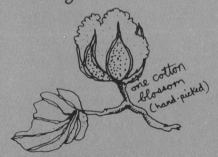

one cotton blossom (hand-picked)

If you had a choice into the past or would you choose? head for the what happened and could travel the future, which I really think I'd future. To see to us all. To see if we made it thru. To know if mankind was able to make real peace with the whole world around us.

These are the kinds of thoughts I've been having lately. The whole entire family has been spending each night down at the drawing hut on the river. Lynne and i climb in the hot Indian sauna while the kids lay out on the hut floor reading books and magazines. I used to have a small sized T.V. but now its gone. Instead we all stare at the fires' burning embers, or drum out deep resonating beats on the old African drum. Sometimes we roast marshmallows or lie back and watch the bats fly around. Mostly it is a place of peace though. You don't have to do anything there. Many times i have simply sat out in the tall grass and watched. Like an animal. Your sight becomes very acute. You see each movement. The wind in the leaves. Squirrels collecting cones for the coming winter. It feels good to just BE THERE.

101

It is so hot that we went to the lake for a swim....

RODEO WEEKEND

This is the Chief Joseph Days weekend. Lots of wild beer drinkers and many cowboys and their horses too.

Shane's best buddy Andy Bottom is here with his sister Emily and then most of lynnes cousins, aunts and uncles. man-seems everywhere you look there's people.

So you know me. mostly i been staying down at my quiet meadow....

But late last night before heading to the tent, i took a long lonely walk over thru all the rodeo livestock chutes, under the rowdy bleachers and to the place where cowboys launch their horses to chase down hapless calves and longhorn steers.

And it was so cool. I was about only 6 inches from all those REAL cowboys and the hairy, snorting horses. So much REALITY!

And probably the coolest sight of all was the lit up tipis. You could see all the indians inside doing stuff.

another one of those strange picture stories by D. PRICE 1996

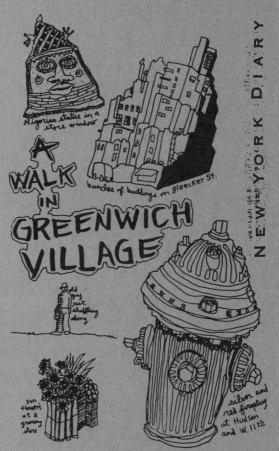

Nigerian statue in a store window

bunches of buildings on Bleecker St.

A WALK IN GREENWICH VILLAGE

old guy just shuffling along

sun flowers at a groovy store

silver and red fireplug at Hudson and W. 11th

CAMPOUT

There's pineneedles in my pockets. All the grass around campsite number two near Summit Peak has been clipped like a golf course by those hungry goats. Mother Natures lawn mowers. They don't require any gasoline. They eat what they mow. What a perfect system. I'm always very jealous of wild animals. They don't have to have homes and clothes and soaps and canned food. They are able to live at base level and carry absolutely nothing extra along.

Just before dropping into a meadow to set up camp i walked up to the metal box on Summit Peak to write my name in the notebook there. I saw that i had visited the same peak exactly 4 years ago.... _TO THE DAY!_ So that got me to dreaming about what i was doing 4 years ago....

... and so we wheeled the old green Dodge right into the Banfield Motel, got a little room right above the swimming pool and walked to the open-all-night Chinese place in Hollywood. We were all laughing and being so crazy. We'd never eaten supper at midnight before......

3x GRASS HOPPER

that Shilo caught
in the garden today.

So as you can see, I've been all over the darn place. And the funny thing is— i haven't even begun to scratch the surface. And that illusive "secret to life", did i find it? Well it didn't take much traveling around to figure out that the best things about life are not out there somewhere, but right where you are, here and now. It really doesn't matter if I'm drawing the Eiffel tower in Paris or this grasshopper in the garden, it's all sacred and worthy of my close attention.

GOOD LUCK and ADIOS!
d.price

draw
COOL
stuff

☆ WATCH FOR NEW ISSUES OF THE MOONLIGHT CHRONICLES TO BE PUBLISHED BY TEN-SPEED PRESS IN THE YEAR 2000.

Chronicle CREED

All us scribes on the friendly planet Earth, promise to continue our sketching ways. On that endless search for <u>TRUTH</u> and <u>BEAUTY</u>. To take big sabbaticals from our busy lives. To live in a simple fashion and be close to nature. To honor our every breath and give huge <u>THANKS</u> for good health, plenty of art supplies, and Shilo's wonderful <u>COOKIES</u>. To truly believe that less is more, but to have one old nice car because we love to travel and be <u>FREE</u>. We pledge to draw and write each day. To be silent and watch the <u>BUGS</u>. To count birds, ride on clouds, and <u>STUDY</u> reality. Oh, and to eat natural foods like mom said. And to only occasionally wear shoes....

multum ..in.. Parvo

'notes

....

....

,...

....

....

....

....

....

....

....

note, 1 nōt; 2 nŏt. **I.** *vt.* [NOT′ED^d; NOT′ING.] To notice; make a note of. **II.** *n.* **1.** A mark; sign; character; annotation; memorandum; brief letter. **2.** Notice; observation. **3.** High importance; distinction. **4.** A character indicating a musical sound; also, the sound. **5.** A written promise to pay.— **note′·book″**, *n.* A book in which to enter memoranda.— **no′ted,** *a.* Well known by reputation or report.— **note′wor″thy**, *a.* Worthy of note.

'notes

· ·

· ·

· ·

· ·

· ·

· ·

pho'to-graph, } 1 fō'to-gråf; 2 fō'to-g̅råf.
fo'to-graf⁸, { It. *vt.* & *vi.* To take a
photograph of; practise photography. **II.**
n. A picture taken by photography.— **pho-
tog'ra-pher,** *n.* One who practises photography.— **pho"to-graph'ic,** *a.* Pertaining
to or produced by photography **pho"to-
graph'i-cal‡.— pho-tog'ra-phy,** *n.* The
process of forming and fixing an image by the
chemical action of light.

109

'notes

draw, 1 drē; 2 drạ, *v.* [DREW, 1 drū, 2 drụ; DRAWN; DRAW'ING.] **I.** *t.* **1.** To pull; haul; lead; attract. **2.** To pull out; extract; call forth; obtain. **3.** To draft: commonly with *up.* **4.** To sketch; portray. **5.** To require the depth of (so much water), as a vessel. **II.** *i.* **1.** To have attractive influence; be attractive. **2.** To have a free draft, as a stove or chimney. **3.** To move as if drawn; as, to *draw* away. **4.** To obtain money, etc., on application. **5.** To delineate, as with a pencil; practise drawing.

stamp, 1 stamp; 2 stămp, *v.* **I.** *t.* **1.** To make by impressing. **2.** To impress by a stamp. **3.** To affix a stamp upon. **4.** To bring down quickly and heavily, as the foot. **5.** To crush (ores). **6.** To stigmatize. **II.** *i.* To strike the foot forcibly upon the ground.— **stamp'er, stamp'ing,** *pa.* & *n.*

stamp, *n.* **1.** A mark made by stamping; device; design. **2.** An implement or machine for stamping. **3.** Kind; sort. **4.** The act of stamping.

|||

'notes

ROAD
RUNNER

na′ture, 1 nē′chur *or* -tiur; 2 nā′chur *or* -tūr, *n.* **1.** The universe. **2.** Inherent or essential qualities; native character; sort; kind.

'notes

art, *n.* **1.** Skill in some practical work;
dexterity; facility; a system of rules; as,
the industrial or mechanical *arts.* **2.** The
embodiment of beautiful thought in artistic forms; also, the works thus produced,
collectively; as, the esthetic or fine *arts;*
also, artistic skill. **3.** Craft; cunning. **4.**
An organized body of trained craftsmen;
a gild.

'notes

sketch, } 1 skĕdh; 2 skĕch. **I**t. *vt.* & *vi.* To
skechʳ, } make a sketch. **II.** *n.* An incomplete but suggestive picture; a short or
incomplete composition; outline.— **sketch'i-
ly,** *adv.*— **sketch'i-ness,** *n.*— **sketch'y,** *a.*

'notes

. . . .
. . . .
. . . .
. . . .
. . . .
. . . .
. . . .
. . . .
. . . .
. . . .
. . . .
. . . .

115

This little book was handrawn by hobo artist d.price, who is

probably this very moment out somewhere chasing the endless line flowing from his pen. Before discovering the romance of art, Price worked as a carpenter, cowboy, cook, grocery guy, waiter, ditch digger, lumberyard truck driver, and ski bum in Sun Valley Idaho. In 1980 he discovered a love for photojournalism and spent 10 years on newspapers in 6 different states. In 1986 he created <u>SHOTS</u>, a fine-art photography journal which he ran for 45 issues. In 1990 he moved to his home state of Oregon to live in a tepee and create his journal <u>Moonlight Chronicles</u>, and hang out with his children Shane and Shilo and their mother Lynne and 7 cats. whew!

d.price

116

Busy guy huh?

woodcarving at shop
• NORTHERN CALIFORNIA •

This entire book was drawn and written with SAKURA PIGMA MICRON pens.